YOU LIVE WITHIN ME..

LILY

Made with ❤ on the Notion Press Platform
www.notionpress.com

To him

To him for whom I wake up every morning,

to him who I miss everytime even while sleeping..

Only my poems can express what I feel for you,

Cuz neither me nor my words can reach you..

Contents

1. Heart in a Rib "Cage"

I don't know,
how it would've been.
If you had still,
been with me.

Maybe we could've shared,
more laughters or maybe more tears.
Maybe if I had a little more courage,
You'd still been here.

But now, with you gone,
nothing feels like before.
Maybe being so attached,
is something I would'nt do anymore.

I wish I had understood befoe,
that I wasn't the only option for you.
You had many others,
but it was me who had only you.

Now that I have learned my lesson,
I wouldn't do the same mistake as before.

Now having understood that I deserve so much better,
I wouldn't look back at you, whatever may be the matter.

You have no idea,
about the state you've left me in.
Maybe because of you,
I wouldn't be able to love again.

2. Sorry

I am sorry for thinking that you were different,
sorry for believing that we'll be together till the end.

I am sorry for being there for you when you needed me,
sorry for guessing that you'd be there when I needed you.

Yea, you did break my heart,
that too when I thought we'd never part.
But when I know that there's nothing that'll ever last,
why did I get attached in the first part?

It would have been way better if we hadn't met,
cus then I would not have to regret.
Regret on why I trusted you,
But now, at any cost, I have to reset.

3. Someone I cherished

It is said,
that life's too short.
And in this life,
you meet many people in a short span of time.

Very mysterious, isn't it?
That roughly out of the 10 people you meet,
you remember only 2.
While the others are forgotten by you.

And out of all your so called besties,
many are probably hating on you.
But you're too sweet to notice that,
and in turn think that they like too too.

Nothing wrong in being sweet, no.
You have your own charm.
But just be careful of those,
who neither deserve you neither your beautiful charm.

What I am trying to say is,
that people come and go in your life.

But just because someone left,
Doesn't mean you'll question your existence.

I am not being melodramatic, no.
I don't want anyone to be glum.
It's just that I know how,
it is to lose someone whom you always wanted to cherish.

4. Broken Promise

Neither were we just friends,
nor were we together.
Neither did we hold hands,
nor did we not confess.

You said you loved me,
like no one ever did.
You said you wouldn't ever stop talking to me,
but that's exactly what you did.

I said I'd be there,
whenever you'd need me.
You said you wouldn't
ever lose feelings for me.

But in the end it's all messed up.
It's neither you starting a conversation with me,
nor replying to any of my texts.

It's all broken in the end.
And as it is,
it's never gonna mend.

But even after all this,
You'll always find the best friend in me.
Which you've probably lost,
since you stopped talking to me.

5. When I saw you happy

Sometimes I feel so lonely,
Thinking no one loves me as much, not even nearly.

I go on day searching for an answer
of where, at which point could I have gone wrong.
But I don't find anything,
rather I start listening to some stupis song.

I want to tell you everything, straight, to the point.
But I end up writing poems like these,
doing nothing but making myself disappoint.

I want those days back,
when I used to cry like hell
and then laugh like nothing happened.
Probably because I knew, you always had my back.

I freaking have no idea what I am doing right now.
Am I looking for an answer?
Am I asking you to come back?
Am I waiting for you to come back?
I just don't want these questions to be true anyhow.

My friends know, how much I cried after you left.
They know how, I couldn't stop feeling what I felt.

You left, never said goodbye, or a single sorry.
I was determined to hate you for eternity.

But I don't know where that hatred went,
When I saw you happy.

6. When I saw you happy (Pt. 2)

When I saw you happy,
I couldn't help but smile.
Probably that's how love is,
you cae for the person no matter how much they made you cry.

You want to see their happiness,
even if that costs you yours.
You keep waiting for them,
when they've forgotten you for years now.

I want you to know I am writing this for you,
I need you to know how much I am in love with you.
I just can't stand the thought that you and me will never have
our ending,
I just can't bear to think who'll hold my hand if it's not you
coming.

You've forgotten me,
I can tell this from miles away.
That's cuz if you did remember,

LILY

You would've atleast wished me on my birthday.

I wasn't even a friend to you, right?
I am pretty sure of it since that's what my heart says.

My heart says millions of other things,
only that they conflict with my mind.
But this one thought, that you love me,
neither crossed my heart, nor my mind.

7. You said you'd stay..

You said you'd stay,
said you'd love to watch me getting married someday.
You said you'd play with me all day,
but you left me mid-way.

I love you,
I didn't tell you this ever, not even once, I remember.
I always wanted you to be with me,
even if it was selfish of me.

Grandparents you were,
you called yourself old.
Kept saying that it was time for you to go.

But I was never ready to say goodbye to you..

I still have the last sweater you made for me,
I still have those cute little socks you made for little me.
I never thanked you enough for them,
when I did, you never responded back.

That night, when you left,

I remember hiding from my mother and crying like hell.
I remember her crying like hell.

You never told us that you were leaving,
rather left us without warning.
You should've given us a little time,
we could've probably changd your mind.

Nothing, Just Love

Not everything has a happy ending,
not everything happens as per the planning.

No one ever loves you as much as to always stay,
No one ever stays even after promising yo wait.

Love comes the way it has to,
Love leaves the way it wishes to.

Not everything has a happy ending,
not everything happens as per the planning.